Here

Also by Sydney Lea:

Poetry
No Doubt the Nameless
I Was Thinking of Beauty
Six Sundays Toward a Seventh
Young of the Year
Ghost Pain
Pursuit of a Wound
To the Bone: New and Selected Poems
The Blainville Testament
Prayer for the Little City
No Sign
The Floating Candles
Searching the Drowned Man

Fiction

A Place in Mind

Essays

Growing Old in Poetry: Two Poets, Two Lives (with Fleda Brown)
What's the Story? Reflections on a Life Grown Long
A North Country Life: Tales of Woodsmen, Waters, and Wildlife
A Hundred Himalayas: Essays on Life and Literature
Hunting the Whole Way Home
A Little Wildness: Some Notes on Rambling

Here

Sydney Lea

Four Way Books
Tribeca

Library of Congress Cataloging-in-Publication Data

Names: Lea, Sydney, 1942- author.
Title: Here : poems / by Sydney Lea.
Description: New York, NY : Four Way Books, [2019]
Identifiers: LCCN 2019004736 | ISBN 9781945588402 (paperback : alk. paper)
Classification: LCC PS3562.E16 A6 2019 | DDC 811/.54--dc23
LC record available at https://lccn.loc.gov/2019004736

This book is manufactured in the United States of America and printed on acid-free paper.

Four Way Books is a not-for-profit literary press. We are grateful for the assistance
we receive from individual donors, public arts agencies, and private foundations.

This publication is made possible with public funds from the
New York State Council on the Arts, a state agency.

We are a proud member of the Community of Literary Magazines and Presses.

For Michael, Beck, Ruthie, Creston, Ivy, Arthur and Cora—beloved grandchildren—and for their parents.

Contents

Here at Summer's End

—for Jerry Dennis

That birds have largely quieted may distress us,

and like neglected mail, the garden's lettuce
went yellow weeks back, then simply dissolved. But we ought to pause
before we focus on loss
in a season still teeming with vegetation.
No matter the month, our sense of wonder remains—
unless we will it to leave.
Even now the mercury flirts with 85,
so it's wondrous, say, how starlings decide
to convene for migration. We can watch their flocks in the roadbeds.

It's a marvel as well, whatever the force is
that's already started to blanch the legs of the snowshoe hares.
Our longing is always for now to endure,
though since the dawn of thinking, many a thinker
has found death an engine of beauty.
Truth is, however, our world will never go dead:
those heads of lettuce have fused with humus below,
and after those starlings wing off, the juncos and titmice will show,
and the ghostly hares of winter

won't be ghosts at all but creatures
with dark flesh packed onto bone under ivory hides.
Coyotes will hunt them to keep alive
through the ineluctable—I almost said awful—chill,
and even then, the ice-beads on softwood boughs may look,
if we want, like permitted fruit. As a season nears,
or lingers, or ends, an amplitude can tell us
we still are subject to spells.
We're here after all. Let's chant it throughout the year

like so much birdsong: we're here we're here we're here

I. Old Lessons

Papillons en liberté

—Montreal Botanical Gardens, May 2014

I'm here with my wife of thirty-odd years
and longing for thirty more. She and I
look below at a riffled pool
that forms from a man-made flume and shines
under man-made light. These butterflies

have hatched in all their many scores.
We watch them dip and rise among
the pool's bright, quick-bursting bubbles.
Spring blooms surround us in pent profusion.
We smile to recall her sister's son,

now far from the small blond child who spoke.
Do butterfries fry good? he asked me.
We repeat the cute old question as one.
In the wild some "fry" 3000 miles.
True, but I almost think it can't be.

They're swept off-course by the paltry air
stirred by visitors' *ahs* and *oohs*.
Still I know it's misguided, the trite equation
of frail and lovely. They're tough. As so often,
fleetingness floors me. And here it shows.

I've learned some names: hello, blue morpho,
and you, rice paper, whom I all but see through,
and postman, you, whose very name
now sounds so quaint, so obsolescent.
Hello-goodbye. How nice to have met you.

Older Age

So much for glory from the morning glories.
Leaves at their margins turn tawny.
I quickly seek other signs—

It's what I do. I'm a poet. The migrant
Flickers gather in byways.
There's a blur of spectral tail-spots

When I flush them, although my driving is slow,
Reactions no longer speedy,
Except for those that are:

Scrawny maples in the swamps have kindled,
There's the first fall warbler—How *dismal,*
I think, *How time goes by,*

As if it were yesterday. And so on.
Yet our neighbor's puppy has doubled
Her weight in just eight weeks.

Old fool, get onto your feet, do something,
Confucius said, *Be useful.*
Winter firewood still needs stacking.

Search Me

—Big Sur, 2015

We're home from the other coast
where only five days back
I instinctively conjured Arnold's
unplumb'd, salt, estranging sea.
Of all the lines. I grasped
his meaning in full but wasn't inclined
to say so, not at least
with my wife and youngest daughter beside me,
for fear of—what would it be?—
estranging them. And yet I wondered:

what comes first: the chicken
of the natural world or the egg of bookish
sensibility?
Do others ponder such things? Search me.
At one point, a seal pricked the surface,
which I longed to think was a shark like Melville's
pale ravener of horrible meat,
though I longed to be more than literary,
and a savage rush from below me
seemed less appalling in any case

than that vast horizontal skyline.
Why should we not enjoy an original
relationship with the universe?
asked the Sage of Concord. Why not indeed?
On our drive to Big Sur, the airwaves
pulsed with lyric cliché until
some deejay announced the death that morning
of B. B. King, whose voice
I've cherished forever, now quieted forever.
In one song, B. B. cried,

I win some battles, but I always lose the war.
I keep right on stumblin' in this
no-man's land out here. And *once*
by the Pacific, Robert Frost
studied the vista I'd been scanning.
He imagined the ocean was scheming
to do something to land never done before.
At length some fractious gulls
banked down upon a skitter of baitfish,
which the seal I saw may have spooked.
Such liveliness suddenly quickened the sea.
Or was that just something I'd read? Search me.

Spilled Milk

—apology to a daughter, almost 40 years late

The train lumbered out of Toronto Station. Together
We headed for subarctic lakes to visit your brother
At camp, your older and only sibling then.
I dreamed of northern air as our coach careened

Past clinkers, barrels, filthy railway sheds,
Ugly as you were lovely. I ordered a spread
Of lunchtime stuff, with for me some coffee, a glass
Of milk for you. A dozen miles would pass

Before you took a drink. You had a habit,
Almost willful, it seemed, of spilling whatever
You drank, and must have been afraid—oh damn it—
To reach for your glass while the dining car swayed and quivered.

As for me, distracted, I was fixed
On the winking waters we'd find upstream from the mess
Of milky river at trackside. In time, we escaped
Those outskirts into open prairie space,

And you spilled the glass. Of course. I pray at least
I said nothing out loud, but I have no doubt you could read

My miserable thoughts. And now if I get to hell—
As I sometimes think I will if justice prevails,

Precisely for things I've thought—my Hadean vision
May be of your shame-ridden, six-year-old face, all riven
By worry, which it should have been my fatherly duty
To soothe, restoring what had been its beauty.

Ukrainian Eggs

I'm off on a late-season fishing trip with the guys.
We bump along in my beat-up pickup, laughing.
Our humor's adolescent, the day bone-chilling.
Meanwhile her dear friend Portia and Robin, my wife,
are learning from Joan, here on a visit, to fashion
Ukrainian eggs. The teacher and students are certain
they'll really be something to see—the eggs, I mean.

After our umpteenth idiot joke, obscene,
I feel some sadness rise up in me like one
a cello might summon. That trio of women back home
Will be chuckling too, I suspect, though their jokes will remain
a lot less crude, no doubt, than ones we're telling.
But the women will also be serious, each intending—
and I'm sure they will—to make objects of beauty and grace.

But why would that cause this weeping response to rise?
Vain male, I turn my face aside. To call
those women cute is absurd. They're not at all
a group that anyone would patronize.
It's perhaps that I'm thinking, and not for the very first time,
how much in my life I would if I could revise,
like the way my grade school posse of punks and clowns

14

would scoff when the girls turned to projects of their own.
Some wore pants under dresses against the cold.
They'd play secretary, nurse or, laughably bold,
even cops, or firefighters, pilots, cowboys, soldiers.
And we—we mocked them, we witless, unschooled fools,
sure of ourselves, sure that we'd always prevail
in that age before we helped to raise our daughters.

Interior

—for Marjan Strojan

Some oddities can settle forever
within a mind—I think of a noise
in my bachelor uncle's cellar,
in the unimaginable, deepest part
where gravel gave way to dirt:

first, an almost inaudible whining,
and then an awful, protracted wheeze,
as of some strange animal fighting
in the gloom to gather its share of air.
I'd make myself stand right there

by the steps to listen, every visit.
Not that I ever dared to walk
across to that recess, hidden
and dark—no, darker than any dark.
My flashlight's puny arc

played on the mouth of what seemed a cavern,
the beast inside now a wolverine,
now something vaguely like a lion
or a scaly dragon from the picture books
by my bed upstairs in its nook.

I still can make my own grim cave
in thought, where hordes of monsters crouch
that could carry my family off.
My ears have tinnitus, constant ringing,
which somehow recalls the breathing

of the dreadful thing. That gruesome sound.
I all but see the enormous snake
that waits for someone alone
like me. The bird flu, SARS, ebola:
all can be bears or bulls or

outsized scorpions, jackals in packs.
And I doubt I'll ever fathom why
one of those picture books,
the one with its clan of peaceful gorillas,
should with each reading have thrilled me

and frightened me so, above all the mother
ape's last words to her infants at evening.
Some oddities live forever.
"Sleep," she told them. "Don't suck your toes,"
which meant the dark was coming.

Gravitas

—for Rick Hausman

I complain to my neighbor I've got no time for another do-good
      committee,
but he insists. He actually tells me I'll bring it some "gravitas."
I block the phone with my palm and snicker, recalling the tormented
      teachers
of My Boyhood, that doomed old republic. How would booze-sick Mr.
      Haas
react to such talk? For him, I invented an author, whose "little known
      works"
I wrote a theme on. He gave me an A. Or Miss Dilson, near bald and
      wattled
math instructor? On the first day of school, I let a grass snake wriggle
out of my backpack onto her floor. Or above all poor Mr. Merrill,

first Latin master, on whom I pulled that slew of idiot tricks.
I guess he must have taught me *gravitas*. The word, I mean.
Would he connect its meaning to the punk who glued his desk drawers
      shut,
who festooned the bumper of his trail-worn Plymouth sedan with a
      string of cans,
and aped him exactly, if I say so myself, for my cynical sect of
      classmates?
Pure cynic too, I relied on his irritation as diversion, impatient

18

as I felt with every lesson. I wince even now to think of that room:
the mustard-colored globe on his desk, its intriguing African nations,

whose names, though I didn't know it, would change; dust puffing from
      the trough of the blackboard;
the soporific *swish* of the janitor's broom along the hallway;
syncopations from the blighted elm whose limb-tips always strummed
a pane when weather blew up from the east; the disheartening bouquet
from the basement kitchen, where invisible workers thumped around as
      they fixed
another bad lunch. I still see Mr. Merrill's eyes as he glowered.
Sometimes I vaguely thought the eyes held something other than fury—
not that I cared. He was just an old man to me, if younger by years

than I am now. Like my father, he'd been in the European Theater,
so that as I write this I suspect he knew things that I had never
      considered
and wouldn't need to in later life. He may even have hoped I wouldn't.
Whatever the case, he must have seen that I could not stay forever
what I seemed to be as I fidgeted there, sullen, restless, ruthless,
desperate to break away from that stuffy third-floor box, that cage,
its never-ending, meaningless *sum, esse, fui, futurus.*
One day I'd understand the look he fixed on me. It was grave.

Children's Fall

—*for Charles Fort*

During lulls in our playground games,
I'd raise my eyes to the blockhouse building
that would close around us soon.
I'd shudder like leaves still barely clinging
to the oaks' bare limbs.

I'd been breathing in autumn mud,
that cherished aroma, and I dreamed of staying
in that dear chill forever,
whooping and darting. Oh, we were just children,
each one of us likely

feeling a private dread.
We all knew we'd soon have to file
as one through that gray stone entrance.
And then the stale room—the math and spelling,
the endless parsing

of those tepid sentences—
all of which felt like a sentence itself,
against which we had no plea.
The season's migrant starlings blathered
and wheezed above us.

Unwilling, it seemed, to leave,
They'd fight the blow, gather a foot,
then lose it again. That flock,
much like our own, had congregated
for a hopeful moment,

then suddenly gave in.
As one, they seemed to recognize
they had no choice but surrender
to forces they owned small means to withstand.
As one, they quieted their clamor,

then went with the wind.

Old Lessons

The metaphor felt so handy it also felt trite:
I wanted my son to depend on me forever
But wanted him too to learn to ride a bike,

First phase of course in a first child's setting out
Away from his father—farther, always farther.
Speed up. Please stop, I thought. Mixed feelings. Trite.

Knuckles pale, he clutched the handlebars tight,
Cried *Hold me! Hold me!* Which needless to say I did
For week after week while he learned to ride a bike.

At last, as one June day slumped into night,
I took my hands away from fender and seat,
And he pedaled off into darkness and distance. Trite,

Looking back, to figure our future lives,
The changes that would come, the way he'd speed
Away on years, as I stood behind that bike.

It's right, of course, that he no longer calls me to hold him—
Have confidence, I remember, was what I told him—
Though it wasn't really a question of riding a bike,
And my feelings, really, were never entirely trite.

The Owl and I

Once the gimcrack cross got burned on our lawn, my mother took off
back north to have me. My father was stationed in Gadsden, Alabama,
before the second great war, commander of so-called Colored Troops,
and he'd invited a few of his men inside the house, it seems,
a radical thing indeed just then in the heart of Jim-Crow Dixie.
So my mother escaped giving birth down there, though I don't have any
     idea
why I'd think of this, which, near to her death, she spoke of so many
     years after.

Why now, on watching a barred owl glide to a hemlock gone dark at
     sundown,
everything else as well going dark around me here where I stand?
Once, at midnight, she thought she'd heard a whoop of human anguish
and wondered whether some soldier was being lynched outside. My
     father
went for a look but found nothing. My lifelong relations with my
     mother
were vexed, I now suspect, in part because between us two
stood a lot in common. Jews were being crammed into cattle cars then,

but for Dad and those troops, the evil in Europe lay several months
     ahead.
Still, real or imagined, that cry of mortal misery stuck with Mother,
though no signs of nearby violence turned up next morning. The company

came en masse to mess: Shit on a Shingle, as the GIs said,
dried beef on toast. So life went on, at least for a while—more or less.
It ought to bring comfort that I'm where I am, aging but safe, my kin
constantly swelling as sons and daughters produce their sons and
        daughters,

and winter, so harsh this year, giving way at last to spring, with
        snowdrops
glinting, the freshets making their evanescent cascades through the
        woods.
I recall how Mother loved this season. Why, then, this lonely sensation?
It feels that I'm in some pitch-black tunnel and won't get out again,
that this, as the saying goes, is it, that all I'll have at the end
—of course there can't be anything to it—is the sorrowful eight-note
        anthem
of that single owl, the sound just now having reached my vexed old
        head,

though I'd be foolish to think that song was addressed to anyone human.

II. Poetic License

No Consequence

—for Goran Simic

A redtail shot from nowhere and killed
One of two black ducklings
Without the least effort as I canoed
A mirror lake at dawn.
When the small bird disappeared, the hen
Rushed to shield the last of her brood,

Urgent as my own mind, which rushed
By habit to metaphor
And by dint of will alone stopped shy
Of the poetaster's *O*—
For all the sad creatures. I paddled on.
So did the two that survived.

They fossicked again for surface insects,
The mother settled her feathers,
The world went ahead with its usual business,
And I thought of my Bosnian friend,
How he opts for a sturdy manner. He tells
Good jokes in the bastard English

He learned from American comic books
And talk behind the translation

Of television sitcom soundtracks.
He moves on. In spite of all.
That poor doomed duckling's wisps of down
Floated in air like snowflakes,

Diaphanous, after the raptor snatched it,
Beautiful, backlit by sun.
I recall the hawk as a totem of splendor
While it managed its own savage business,
Even as the pitiable rasps and squalls
Of the grown duck likewise linger,

Indelible, in the brain. And so
I may just write of them soon,
Though I think how my friend beheld the brain
Of a better friend splayed against
A wall in a town so picturesque
It all but beggars the mind.

O, I'm a poet of no consequence.
The sniper picked one of two
Who walked a quaint old street together.
I feel guilt, not envy. It's true:
I'm content enough in life to be
So wanting in subject matter.

News Comes Third

Oh, these guilty pleasures, if that's what I really should call them.
I buy the local paper and my usual cup of store coffee,
Then drive back home and sit, ignoring whatever may be
Transpiring outside the window: squall of a spring tom turkey
Calling his hens, the contrails of planes on their way to Europe,
Tokyo, Rio, Paris. Who cares? I sip from the cup,
And turn first thing to letters, primarily to see

Just what might annoy me today. If it's someone fussing over
An issue like water rates in a small town near or far,
Whose fortune or misfortune I have no personal stake in,
I go right ahead to the sports. I check how my teams are doing.
That is, if I haven't spent the preceding evening's hours
Watching games on TV. What the hell? I'm retired, so leave me alone.

My wife was right upstairs, likely watching stuff of her own
Like some period thing from Great Britain, which would lull me to sleep
in an instant.
No, give me two on and two out in the bottom of the ninth,
An impossible, game-clinching shot in overtime, a field goal
From fifty yards out. I don't care if some lady whines in her letter
How the clerk in a local shop, when she asked him for help, said *Forget it,
I'm busy.* That woman claims that people were kinder once,

But I bet that complaint was heard when people still lived in caves.
Don't tell me my wife and I should hone our "communication."
We know each other like twins. We've been lovers for almost four decades.
Can you tell me you're doing better? A train shakes the valley each
       morning
While I'm feeding my sports addiction. I don't mind that sound far away.
News comes third, and it seems these days it's always a mess.

(There I go sounding myself like that woman I just made fun of.)
Another exotic disease. Another IED.
A register man shot dead by someone less nice than the lady
Upset by a rude clerk's behavior. I go back and skim through recaps—
Never mind if I've seen the game, above all one that we've won,
Though for me to say *we* is absurd, and don't think I don't know it.
I'm sure there's not one player who'd give me the time of day.

Though I've never met her, I don't like to think of that letter writer
Because I'll start making a picture: her husband dead in the Gulf,
Her kids all disappointments or worse—on drugs or in jail
Or both. She stares through tears out her shit-box apartment window
While I read such letters and fume or check the stats and the box scores.
I keep my eyes off the photos that go with the news, which comes third.

Chimera

The eagle's wings were angled
In a stoop that seemed almost languid,

And yet in an eye-blink it flew
Past the window and out of view.

For me, now in my seventies,
It can feel as if everybody

Were gone, or about to be gone:
For instance, my brother-in-law,

dead some time now, young.

I loved him for years and years.
Parents. A sibling. Peers.

The great creature's cutting across
The window: less sight than loss,

As if flight had exemplified
The concept, *brevity,*

And the bird were conscious of me,
And consciousness were crucial

In you or me or an eagle.

Machu Picchu

A younger friend and his lovely wife from Peru
want to lead a community hike through the mountains there.
I've always dreamed of going to Machu Picchu.
I keep on dreaming that I'm still 24.

We're at our pal Marv's old fishing shack on Cape Cod,
its stairway so steep I'm glad there are railings to cling to.
My knees are 73 years old as I write.
God knows, I'll never climb to Machu Picchu.

I have six little grandchildren now. I had to stay
alive this long to love them. The youngest one
is ten months old, near walking. There are seals in the bay
each time we friends go fishing. Today at dawn,

I watched a sanderling flit to the beach and nab
a hermit crab. There's a loud osprey nest by the landing.
Soon the chicks will fly off, on their own, but come to that,
why haven't they done so already, October looming?

Truth is, I can't say. I can't say why they're still there.
I had to stay alive this long to know
all I don't know and what little I do. I've stayed
behind this evening while the others go looking for blues.

I won't reach Machu Picchu. There are thousands of things
I'll never accomplish. The news says thousands will perish
in Syria. Starvation and worse. Through a windowpane
I see Virginia Creeper choking a larch,

whose needles all have yellowed. Later on,
they'll fall with the season. I can't find words to render
justly the beauty of the long vine's leaves as they turn,
how the cold-dimmed edges frame blazes at their centers.

Little Squalls

To stand at the sink drying dishes feels routine,
Except that the sun seems to drop too quickly,
Like a china plate he might fumble.
He can all but sense the crash, if not with his ears.
His wife just left on a trip to a far-off city.

Her exit, that sunfall: they engender a mild inner ruckus.
Running late, she offered too brief a goodbye.
Her taillights plunged down the lane—
Though the day isn't yet full dark—like odd little comets.
He wants her back before she's well out of sight.

For whatever reason, he recalls having tripped on a trail
This morning, and feeling the lancet-like prick
Of a dead underbough near an eye.
It appeared a sort of wonder: he'd been spared for the moment,
Which made him silently say, *I ought to direct*

My thanks somewhere. But rather he stood clod-still,
The same as now, moving only a thumb
To tamp his tiny wound.
His response was far from distinctive—he thought
How fragile things were. He couldn't stare up at the sun,

But in mind he watched it gallop down the heavens.
Closer by, a phoebe wobbled a bough
While the woods-floor's springtime smells
Blended with ones of a winter not quite subsided.
His blood made the same commotion in him as now:

Two times in a day.
                    The bird's waving tail showed no greeting.
It wasn't eternal, married love.
New sap would drip into duff.
How deluded he's been, he concludes, for ever believing
Dear things can last, or would—if they could—be enough.

I Keep Going at 20 Below

It's too cold for me to stay out long at my age,
so I trek the half-mile road below our shed,
its earth deep-hidden beneath the white.
Far east, Black Mountain shows up, starkly edged
on a sky full of crystals. My boots on frigid ground
are cheeping loudly enough that with these bad ears
I can't right off discern another sound:

pine siskins by the score. They yammer from every
evergreen in sight. I used to plow
on snowshoes through powder, hour on hour.
It shames me to say that the notion scares me now.
Still it's hard to keep with wistfulness when air
keeps glittering so, and creatures no bigger than thumbs
keep at their sustenance, dauntless. Each bird tears

at bough-tips, feeding and tweeting. I focus on one
that worries the sparkling tip of a spruce-cone, eats,
then darts to another.
                              Beyond the bird,
beyond the conifers in which it sat,
beyond the outlying mountain—well, what passes
even beyond bright air? And who's to sense it?
Not I. It's birdsong that prompts such opening phrases.

Beyond all this, let time complete my sentence.

I Impugn a Victorian

There are a thousand thoughts lying within a man
that he does not know till he takes up a pen to write.
—William Makepeace Thackeray (1811-1863)

Or within a woman. Or maybe
old Thackeray was delusionary, yearning
to believe that, simply by being a writer, he could write
and thoughts would just show up. It's been too long since I read
about his Becky Sharp and others to evaluate whether in fact they do
arrive in his famous *Vanity Fair* or elsewhere in the eminent Victorian's
    work.

Maybe he's only vain. But I also yearn to believe
that, reading that passage somewhere, I jotted it down
because somehow its words spoke to something inside me.
That is, now that I'm taking up the pen's contemporary equivalent—
now that I'm writing, I hope my scribbles will appear, perhaps, not as
    thought
precisely, but as subject or theme that will ring the least bit true. At least
    I can dream so.

Or, on a better day, if you'll forgive my presumption,
they may even instruct. How long, however, dear William,
must I keep on composing these lines without deliberation
before the thoughts you speak of supervene? I'd settle for one.

It's exacting to keep all this up, dimly expecting some higher level
of mental engagement as, meanwhile, the feeder by our window teems

with the same old delightful birds of our winters:
redpoll, pine siskin, minuscule brown creeper, nuthatch,
the usual horde of chickadees, a tufted titmouse, hairy and downy
woodpeckers, and now and again, to the more alert birds' consternation,
and mine—though I confess its beauty also thrills me—a sharp-shinned
     hawk.
Fixed on murder, it skulks in the high bare limbs of that paper birch
     until it stoops

upon some blithe little victim, or, more curiously,
merely perches there, declining to dive and to wreak
its havoc. Your comments have made little peace in my mind,
Mr. Makepeace. I took you at your word and here I am, less far along
thought's avenue than I was at the start. I've been pressing and prosing
     ahead
for five desultory stanzas, and I conclude, since I have to move toward
     conclusion,

that like so much of life in the way I have known it,
all but a tiny part of the process has consisted of waiting
without a clue. Not that there isn't a whole array of worse
concerns to fret about than this bemusement. I haven't yet gone down

to the village store to fetch the newspaper, doubtless full of examples of
       such
worse things. But meanwhile: Look at all these birds—so vivid,
       brilliant—who etch

their small and eloquent marks upon the snow,
even the ones without a clue they're close to death.

—for Bob Demott

Stoicism

Through a frost-flowered pane I watch his truck disappear,
Sole moving thing in a wide tableau
So still with cold it might be an abstract painting—
White on white—
And under that pall, hunkered in terror,
Small harmless creatures seek cover from ravening foes.

The huge man gulped his coffee, then he scampered
From our wood-warmed kitchen. He's here for a week
While he takes a course not far from his childhood raising.
He dare not be late.
He'll soon be a wilderness first responder,
An apt description: that son has always been quick

To ease whatever pain he can in others.
As for me, when the same week's end arrives,
I'll take one more step from seventy toward my eighties.
Should I celebrate?
Until then, our son will train in weather
Stalled for some time at zero degrees, or just shy.

I can't hide, of course, from predator age forever.
Nobody does, I remind myself.
The fact that I've survived this long is maybe
No more than fate.

My father fell, and one of my brothers,
Too young. I picture our child knee-deep in drifts.

For hours today, he'll study lifesaving measures
Against near-drownings, cuts to the bone,
Hypothermia, ski crashes, shivered limbs.
How the hours have raced
Since he, blond boy in grass-stained trousers,
Tore breathless up from our field that afternoon

And into the kitchen with a handful of bluets so tender
That before he could bring them inside they'd shriveled.
Mom and Dad, he blurted in sheerest delight,
His words a spate:
Look what I did! I picked you flowers!
If I permit myself so much as a sniffle
Just now, the tears behind it will follow for hours.

What's to Be Expected?

One evening before Youth Fellowship I found
Some organ pipes on the floor and knelt beside them,
singing "Long Tall Sally" into one. Meanwhile,
I signed my name with a finger in the dust
of the nubbly concrete. No one had ever done
these things all at once—and no one ever would.
That was a fusty basement room in St. Paul's.

Why this recollection on the bank of a brook?
Less strange to remember a poem by Robert Frost,
whose brook runs out of song and speed come June.
The one I stand beside has never sung,
has never run. It barely crawls at ice-out,
and by now, mid-May, its water has seeped to nothing.
What's new? Not much. It does this every year.

Snow melts, the freshets goad it, then it dies.
The barn opposed across the way. . . . But enough
of Frost, irrelevant here, where a barn is crumbling
in that field of weeds. It needs refurbishment
that it won't get. The sills are rotted, walls
all splayed like a doomed doe's legs on ice.
Did someone stand on its earthen ramp with a golf club?

Unlikely. So how on earth did that dimpled ball,
egg-like below me, land in its nest of dried algae?
Nothing's to be expected or ever was.
Consider any two people, supposedly normal,
and prepare yourself to hear of odd behavior.
One may raise chinchillas, one love tango.
We wonder, *Who'd expect it?* Answer: no one.

I labored to be unique when I was young,
but what of my uncle, who'd listen to *The Ring
of the Nibelung* while plucking his geese for the larder?
It was just what he did, not striving to be eccentric.
His brother, my father, served a tough stint in the army,
European Theater, World War II.
So why did he love to sing old Navy tunes?

Search me. Search him. He much preferred fresh water.
I smell his bay rum now as I recall him,
and contemplate a ball in withered muck,
and note a certain barn, gap-toothed, neglected,
and conjure Robert Frost, great local author,
and remember an uncle, a basement, Little Richard:
now what, I ask you—what's to be expected?

Gooka-mol

To watch that band of vultures
coast along their thermal this morning
is to marvel at elegance and composure.
There's no need to repress old platitudes
about the birds as tokens
of doom. I don't even take up the notion,

or rather, if I did,
I'd imagine the doom of some woodland creature.
No, why not be honest? My mind's on our dog.
Just last week, the vet saw a bulge
she didn't like on his chest.
Tomorrow she'll cut it out. At a loss,

I think of the vultures' circling.
I think of etymology,
how some people call those birds *revolting*,
which literally means they turn us away,
how *vulture* itself in fact
derives from the verb for *turn* in Latin.

I'm thinking, you see, of whatever
has nothing to do with a horrible illness.
Shrecklich, I name it, recalling my grandmother's
Pennsylvania Dutch locutions,

which I probably can't even spell.
Sometimes she'd cry out *Gooka-mol,*

which signified *Let me see.*
Cancer's taken far too many
beings who've shared their lives with me.
The dog has set my mind on this course,
and I think to myself, *Gooka-mol,*
as the string of birds slips over a knoll.

Where have they gone? I can't say.
From the height that the birds command, I might
look down on someone behaving this way
and simply conclude, *The man is crazy.*
It's only a pet, after all,
and the world's still wide and rich and lovely.

Granted. It is. Sometimes. *Gooka-mol.*

Poetic License

—for Fleda Brown

She appeared to be standing hock-deep in a cove,
her eyes on each flash of my blade.
I paddled in for the thrill of watching a wild thing's flight.
When the doe didn't run, I concluded she couldn't.

I circled to view the ruined hindquarters,
the entrails that fluttered like pennants in slow-moving water.
She wasn't standing at all
but knelt in the dusk of ash and cottonwood shade.

I returned to the launch and started over,
intent on a personal best
to the bridge upstream and back in the light,
long kayak I use whenever I race.

At my age, of course, my real competition
is time itself. I kept my eyes from the cove
as I passed again, yet resist as I might,
I felt off-course, not because of the fate of the doe,

which I knew to be common, or at least scarcely tragic,
except as the sentimental apply the term.
Not that I didn't hope the coyote
would come back to end the deer's struggle,

or that she'd weaken and drown
before I came back myself from upriver.
No, my true distraction lay in thinking a poem
might be struggling its way to the front against my will.

I'm strong, if I say so, at least for my age,
and if I hadn't drifted ever so briefly
to see her still kneeling, I'd surely have made my best time yet.
Not strong enough to stay honest, however, I sensed

old art prevailing. (Pardon the precious diction.)
How fitting, I thought, if sunlight could turn now to rain,
It didn't, but that hardly mattered.
I had license to choose from a store of old lies,

full access, that is, to a whole range of skies.

.

III. A Tide Like Grace

Irresolutions

Our dog was not used to a leash.
I should have been holding the dog.
The squirrel was used to leashed dogs.

The dog chased the squirrel to the end of the leash.
The squirrel seemed all but indifferent.
The dog is a strong yellow Lab.

She pulled my wife off her feet.
My wife broke her collarbone.
It was our granddaughter's birthday.

I should have been there at the party.
Our family had gone to a park.
I was in North Dakota.

I should have been holding the dog.
My bones are more tough than my wife's.
Next day her little dog died.

Not the one that caused the trouble.
No, the poor old blind-deaf spaniel.
He'd always been her special pet.

Our son drove from his place to our place.
He took his mom and her dog to the vet.
I'm the one who should have done that.

Our son had just bought a house.
He and his wife were excited.
It was very unselfish to do what he did.

Our son dearly loves his mother.
I love her too beyond words.
It should have been I who drove her.

A man shot eight people soon after.
That mess was way out in Alberta.
I can be grandiose.

I can dream up phony connections.
I can think all bad things my fault.
I should still have been holding the dog.

Such killings don't normally happen up there.
But this was the second this year.
Such things shouldn't happen anywhere.

Two of the dead were young children.
Then the man turned the gun on himself.
"This is awful for us" said the chief of police.

The gun was a 9-mil Glock.
It had been stolen eight years before.
But the murders went down last month.

So did my poor wife's harm.
Meanwhile I stood there or sat.
I paced and cursed and did nothing.

And what might I have done?
It's five a.m. on New Year's.
I should have found something to do.

I've been thinking of choices I've made.
I can think they have mammoth effects.
I should have been holding the dog.

I think they mean more than they do.
I'm often so grandiose.
There's an oft-quoted James Wright poem.

It ends "I have wasted my life."
My reasons for thinking that differ from his.
In the grand scheme my choices mean nothing.

Having no choice I accept as much.
My wife once hung up a magnet.
Let go or be dragged it said.

I'm physically stronger than she is.
I'm not so otherwise.
I should have been holding the dog.

Fire and Jewel

Eighty-foot hemlock, spruce, fir, pine—
They kept lifting off their stumps like so many rockets,
smoke trails and all. And I
beheld the fire cross-lake from where I drifted.

I'd been plumbing the water for fish when my eyes were lifted.
Fifty years later, I still recall my thoughts,
and how I felt that to think them was more than odd:

I was glad I had faculties to behold
the hill's astonishing orange heat as it flared
to white with each explosion,
then the whole of the conflagration bending toward earth,

a horizontal wall, a monolith
that somehow tore downhill in a sudden fury
of wind. It was gorgeous. Several hours would go by

till I learned Earl Bailey was forced to fly
as quickly as he could on his 'dozer down
from the ridge right into Farm Cove.
He just had to take the loss. It was that or burn.

Donald Chambers, wielding an axe in his turn
with the makeshift crew, collapsed from labor and heat.
Paul the storekeeper dragged him away by his feet.

I knew Don, sadly, just a few more years.
He and Earl and Paul: good honest men.
I can't account for dreams
like the one last night when I watched that fire again.

In what seemed again pure quiet, serene,
the same jetliner as years ago crossed high.
The same scent rose—torched needles, caustic smoke.

The same evil roar came on as I rocked
in the same canoe, the waves still slapping its hull.
In an hour, five decades back,
the length of that ridgeline turned the color of onyx.

The latest of my wife's birthdays will soon be upon us.
Is that why the dream passed smoothly into the next one?
I saw, precisely, a beautiful onyx stone,

hung on her breast from a slip of chain.
I'd never dreamt such a woman as that hillside blackened,
wouldn't meet her for years. Today,
I drove to a jewelry shop, as if still dreaming.

Three hundred miles to the west of that little mountain,
I bought the necklace and felt some fire in my being,
mild version of one that kindled in that old autumn,

which has for a long time, underground, kept burning.

Cavaliers

From up here, the valley looks dazed
with spring, and whatever I see
seems a gift. Meanwhile, so help me, I wonder
why I've never known a thing
about cribbage. Not that it mattered,
but back in the ward, my wraith of a roommate,
ninety-two years old,
had set up a game to play
with his daughter, who told him they could both keep at it
until baseball came on TV.

I gave a huff of relief,
not too loud, I hope, well pleased
to know a change was coming
from all those fatuous game shows,
the volume turned to headache pitch,
the old man's droop-lobed ears
even weaker, I guess, than mine.

I lay there fettered: oxygen hose,
monitor, saline IV.
I'd had some chest pains that morning.
Three drawings of blood, all hours apart,
were apparently needed to prove
I'd suffered no *event*.

And so, worse luck, I was going to be stuck
for a night with this poor old guy.
The daughter kept saying, "Be patient."
though he'd been in that room for over a month.

So the two of us watched the Red Sox,
who kept getting by on breaks,
passed balls, bloops, and walks, and squeaked
a victory out in the ninth.
We whooped until he coughed
so hard I rang my buzzer. A nurse
came in and frowned and pinned him.

He choked down a potion that killed
the hack. He fell asleep, but all night
he'd jerk awake and shout,
"Is anybody out there?"
How long, I mused, can a person be patient?
I couldn't say. I'd be gone
early the following morning,
my diagnosis, at least for now—
mere heartburn. So now I've scrabbled
up a hands-and-knees ridge to rejoice

in a seemingly healthy heart. The world
as I say looks suffused with grace.
There's the scent of melting snow,
muddy soil, wet duff. Gray frogs
are clucking in vernal pools,
the freshets jingle downhill,
woodpeckers rattle the air, new growth

lights up the tips of boughs,
the sky is far more vivid
than what we settle for naming *sky-blue*.
So why should I think about cribbage?
No matter. Before I set out,
I had to look it up, researching,
old-style, in a reference book.
As I read, I heard the clanks
of gurneys, alarm bells that spoke
of souls who were trying to rise from beds

that they were meant to stay in.
I can hear the clamor now,
even these miles and hours away.
Cribbage, it seems, was invented

by John Suckling, near-forgotten
seventeenth-century writer and peer,
said to be "carefree and witty,"

features of poets called Cavaliers.

Gratitude

Our old dog threw up today
nothing new or convenient
I kept myself from cursing
she didn't mean to do wrong
true some words pushed at my lips
but I recalled the psalmist's
caution on the loosened tongue

to describe it too mildly
wrath can be too enticing
a tongue is hard to govern
harder than ship or blood horse
says the scripture I summoned
I thought that of the seven
deadly anger might be worst

though I do leave room for pride
which is kin but my odd calm
seemed to me a miracle
the poor dog looked so contrite
nothing she'd done was her fault
now I must go to the vet's
the thawing wind came last night

bringing other things to do
snow slid off our metal roof
into a mass on the drive
which needs to be cleared away
a job I truly despise
but there is where duty lies
and there's where I need to be

I always wanted somehow
to be elsewhere who knows where
earth is a good place for me
sometimes I snicker at how
coaches say they want their teams
to play *one game at a time*
what in hell else would they do

play two three or four at once
but I've been likewise silly
in my crazy history
I take one day at a time
I seek an easy does it
stance toward life on this planet
death once beckoned me and I

rushed there I won't give detail
opiate   cutter   gunfire
poison gas   race   infernal
these were some crossword problems
I pondered last night in bed
of course they weren't connected
except it was I who saw them

together I solved just three
before sleep overcame me
I did not feel frustration
nor too much inner protest
I know our dog will be fine
I know I'm a lucky man
I'm grateful for peace and rest

I spoke an awkward prayer
if that's in fact what it was
I only spoke it within
and in ignorant belief
that it might just land somewhere
I thanked some hidden power
that I never carved my life

quite to hell nor did I race
to needle blade pistol gas

The 21st Century

She could pull the knob at the end of the string.
Why didn't she think of it sooner? She could drag down the folding
       ladder
and climb up there. Then she'd lie dead quiet
in the yellowed baby clothes and sheets
she's meant to bag up forever to drop at the church's thrift shop,
if someone could please explain
when in the world she'd scare up time,

what with working and keeping house. If she lay still enough, who'd find
       her?
She could take up some apples, some wine.
She pushes away the breakfast pots—
covered with crust and goo she'll have to scratch off—
and rests her head on her elbows. She almost sleeps
and almost smiles, remembering something sweet.

She daydreams back to what now seems long ago.
2010. Her dress wasn't white
like most she's seen. It had this cute little tint of pink.
He showed the whole party how he could make
a circle nearly around her waist
with his thumbs and middle fingers. He was big, she figured, but gentle.
He'll pick up Sue and Michael

from day care coming home.
She never thought she'd be glad she stayed in school,
if you can call it glad.
She fought like a cat with her mom over that.
He's all I want, she screamed—and kids: one boy, one girl.
She's got it all now. These days she scarcely leaves
her chair at work except to pee.

She learned enough to be able to make
a service book for these foreign toaster ovens
out of stuff she punches up on her screen.
But once the book's together, what's it supposed to mean,
at least to her? How will it change her life?
The kids are four and two, and it's like
they hate each other's guts, which her nosy mother says
is only a normal phase.

Does that mean she has to like it?
Whining and snot and laundry. And why don't they ever run
to *him?* It's not like he's evil.
He's a pretty good guy in fact. She looks
at the oversized kitchen clock,
its face all painted with little birds
that squawk and jabber and coo. They all take turns

on the hour. He'll be singing now, that lousy nuthatch.
All she knows about a nuthatch
comes from the clock. It's a horrible, grinding whine
so ugly and nasty she supposes the sound
is not the real one in nature. Soon they'll all be here.
She wouldn't stay long, maybe twenty minutes—
with her shoes off, a little drunk—

smelling clean camphor there in the attic.

Annie's Duck Sauce

I must be prepared to sit
for hours. For me, that's fine;
we will speak heart-to-heart, or just chat.
The main ingredient's time.

Because Annie's 89
when she tells me how I should mix
molasses, spices, soda,
duck drippings and orange zest,

some of her part of the talk
concerns elders, needless to say,
whom she often recalls with humor
but as often with elegy.

She too has gone away
as I summon the recipe,
and yet she appears as the minutes
crawl and the fixings seethe,

redolent, dark as tea.
Her uncle George MacArthur
made railroad ties with an ax.
Her father Franklin skippered

the venerable steamboat *Robert
S:* once ice had broken,
she towed great booms to the river,
then men drove the logs to the ocean.

The pan, cast iron, old-fashioned.
is one Annie handed to me
no more than a few months after
her brother passed away.

That brother and I crouched to wait
for the ducks of a favorite slough.
We never told anyone which.
We haunted that place, we two.

But I was speaking before
of Annie, who, as I listened,
seemed almost a force of nature,
optimistic, insistent

on the good in any person,
in the meanest one in existence,
or the saddest situation.
At last the sauce has thickened.

These days dear Annie's a figment.
She's gone. She isn't here
to test the spice in the mixture,
which causes my eyes to water.

I could have listened all year.

Auction

If I passed their sway-backed house on a summer day,
like anyone in town I'd hear Fred scraping
at his cherished rosewood fiddle,
which is now just char.
Hazel would be singing, no better than her husband played.
Neither one cared. They made their music for fun—
and I made fun of them both.
Then came fire.
I feel odd guilt to consider their frailty,
and I wonder, *What am I here to see?*

ii.

Out of nowhere I think of an early love,
of how often I laughed at her dreams of being a painter,
at what she hoped but was simply unable to save
with shapes on canvas and colors.
Of course she left me.
My life has been more capacious than I deserve,
but in those days, how loss kept scorching my soul!
I was all but speechless. She later died of an illness,
horribly, young.

I reflect that after her fire for me
had cooled and soon in fact simply guttered,
I sometimes wished catastrophe would strike her.

iii.

Fred and Hazel, reduced to cinder:
that was a shock and a shame.
But more vanished too, some even beforehand.
The children they bred in that old house
had moved far off years back,
though they've come today to reap what little they may.
Their son and two daughters are here,
unlike the initialed silverware;
the tunes we mocked;
crude watercolors Fred wrought of sunsets,
snowstorms, birds, old barns, and deer;
Hazel's antimacassars—
black wisps on blackened couch and chair;
old photographs of his parents and hers,
long gone, now gone again. And again
I'm thinking of goneness,
the way my lover would dip the brush in paint

and scowl, as if in pain.

Here, so little remains to sell, it's absurd.

The auctioneer stumbles, searching for words.

All Hallows' Eve

I hollow my body out before bed:
contacts, partial denture,
hearing aids. Blurry-eyed, gap-toothed,
aching and hard of hearing,
again I thank an unnamable something
for what I have. However
dim in my sight it may be, the water
in our pond downhill still reaps
the burnish of the rough-edged moon that winks
through the same old window tree.
Remarkably like a pack of dogs,
between the ridges that make a frame
for our same old house,
the barred owls yammer.

Downstairs, our three real dogs
snuff and twitch in dream.
One child's out west, and how I pray
she doesn't love it. I love her,
and the other six who live nearby.
No doubt *their* children trick or treat.
At last, before I lay me down,
I attempt some re-assembly:
two wrist braces for carpal tunnel,
collar-pillow, CPAP mask

lest tonight be the one when I breathe my last.
Like a jack-o-lantern, that ghostly creature
grins ear to ear
in the dresser mirror.

Aesthetics

Tuesday. Somewhere I'd guess around the 4000th
one of my life, and I'm washing my coffee pot
and putting it onto the dish rack, the way I've done
every Wednesday too, every Thursday, every Friday,
Saturday, Sunday, Monday for many years—

most of the 74 by now—so there's nothing
you'd refer to as thought in the process, and then out the window
—*whoosh*—like a breathtaking comet, in broadest daylight
a broadwing hawk swoops in and scatters the finches
from our feeder, which, however we try to stop them,

draws squirrels as well, both red and gray. It's a gray one
the hawk has his eye on, and the hawk up close seems big
as a goose, though he's lithe and deft and incredibly quick
in his stoop. He misses, however, his quarry cart-wheeling
under a stunted pine I've meant for ages,

again and again, to chop to better the view
through this same kitchen window. And now, as after all
something you might call thought returns, I wonder
if I'm glad I left the tree upright. The hawk was lordly,
just like the one my wife reported seeing

last week, which started an almost identical dive
but flared up the ridge when he found no game out there
among spilled seeds, where the blood on wet March snow
would have shown so gorgeous, so brilliant in either case.
The look of the writhing, dying squirrel would have been pathetic,

no doubt of that. The world's a puzzling place.

A Tide Like Grace

—for Stephen Arkin

I've soaked up my portion of sorrow.
But then who hasn't? Mine can't compare
with some, I know. Take Molly, not even a grownup,
driving her dad's ragtop Olds,
reduced lifelong to muteness and wheelchairs
when that truck ran a light. We all could name such loss.

Foolhardy, I kayaked across
wide water today, and out on that bay,
I found welter, confusion—endless salt waves racing
from north and south and elsewhere
because of two big ferry boats' wakes.
It was hard to imagine where I'd do best to steer.

No matter. I'm still here.
For some reason, I dwelt on my melancholy
over absences as I paddled—brother, parents,
schoolmates, friends and mentors—
though I knew my pain paled next to a Molly's.
I even thought of a long-gone pony I grieve for,

her four hooves thrust toward the rafters,

my boyhood mare Miss Prim, all bloated

from deadly nightshade. My thoughts ran from grand to petty,

you see, as I rode those swells.

I should have been focused on where I floated,

though my course for the most part seemed beyond my control,

as it always has. Truth to tell,

it was tide, like grace, that brought me to shore,

where I spoke aloud, in wonderment: *I'm here.*

—Woods Hole, 2014

Memo for 2027: A Love Poem

—for Robin, forever and always

Dear Self,

If you have lingered through the next ten years, then please look back
And think of me kindly. I'm the one who sought against
All odds to set you straight. It took some doing, yes,
But after that set-to with the tail-gating driver, just for instance,
When, although I was over sixty, I challenged him face to face
(No matter he was big and young and wore that headband
Marked, so it seemed, with smears of blood, his own or someone's)
And he backed down and, squealing his beater's tires, drove
Away from the corner by the general store where I had stopped,
To the amazement of townspeople looking on, to stare him down,
The careless bastard. . . . It took some doing, but I resolved
To learn from that incident, one of the countless, that only remorse

Can ever follow from that sort of behavior, "justified"
Or otherwise, and from that resolution to teach you
Forbearance like that young man's, if that's indeed what it was.
And will I have taught you, say, that fussing with your grandchildren,
As it had been when your very own children were helpless and small,
Was in the end a matter of little kids in a huff
With one another? Will you be able to lift your eyes
From such pettiness and look to the hills and count your blessings,

Even if you can't climb those hills as even I
Can do, however slowly, now? Let me tell you:
Those hills are full of wonder. How flawed and blind you were,
Back then when you were me. I can only hope that the hills

I'm talking about will abide, even if you do not.
I'd like for instance to know I could pass along to you
The way late winter's sun makes wondrous shadows on
The snow out there, as well-groomed little songbirds hop
From seed to seed while just above their heads in the shrubs
Others peck and fret and glance around and show
The gorgeous, shadowlike striations on their wings,
But mostly, I hope you may still behold the generous wife
Who stands some little distance off from those birds and smiles,
First at them and their antics and then through the window at me,
And if she does, then I advise—no, I command—
That you bring down those eyes from those lovely hills so that they fix

On her, and count *that* blessing, maybe count it more
Than all the indisputable others you've been shown.

IV. The View in Late Winter

A Grandson Sleeps on My Chest

The thread of drool from his lip to my shirt
shows lovely, prismatic, refracting the beams
of this fine warm April sun as I loll on a couch.
Those colors won't blend with the song
from the classic country station I just tuned in.

Hank Williams is just so lonely it damned near kills him.
There's a dog asleep too, in a circle of light
on the rug, near a pair of rattles, a teething ring,
and a bear that his late great-grandmother
made by hand years back for this sweet child's father.

Oh I could get going on how that father,
our son, has become such a good big man
when only yesterday, as the cliché has it,
I held him just this way.
Oh I could get going all right about the absence

of the sweet-mannered woman who fashioned the bear,
twice the size of this boy in my arms.
I could fret again that maybe I've come up short
as man or parent or husband,
but no, I won't be going that way, or those.

Hank's midnight train is whining low
while here I hear only lyrical breathing
and the odd and oddly comical infant gurgle.
A scent from the grandson's crown
wafts up. That's when all preachments waft up too,

all vanities, worries, to die their sudden deaths.

The Long and Short

Betty, as always, was making doughnuts.
Why would she stop, I supposed, even though
Her husband had died two nights before?
A few general stores would keep buying her stuff.
People loved those doughnuts, plain as they were.

I could tell she was cooking before I knocked
By smelling her obsolete deep fryer.
I'd known them forever. No storybook marriage,
But she and Dale for the most part got on,
The way old couples usually manage.

Grease-smoke fused with that wet-dog smell
In the woods, which signals we'll soon get snow.
Two flickers flushed near their neighbor's trailer.
Dale was gone. He'd been here and now he was gone.
I pictured his walk, how he reeled like a sailor

After a long-log rolled off a truck
Years back and turned one knee to dust.
A three-legged chipmunk ducked under a downed
Dead hemlock. I watched a pigeon slip
Inside the loft of their spavined barn.

They felt fitting, these varied signs that boded
Winter. Mind you, I *did* like Dale,
And would miss him all right. Yet I caught myself,
Surprised and ashamed, in a sort of rehearsal
Of poignant recall for Betty, and grief,

No matter a small brook cheerfully chimed
A hundred yards off, no matter the field,
Which their neighbor had planted with rye for cover
Through the coming cold, looked green as spring.
Betty called me in. She was leaning over

Her basket. She smiled and wept at once,
And the tears fell down to the bubbling oil,
And they hissed and stuttered and danced inside.
Our years now seemed both long and short.
"*They're* lively anyhow!" she cried.

Stick Season

—for Peter Gilbert

The one that precedes my season is the one that always shows
in those quaint calendar photographs, the one that brings the tourists
to scenes that are glorious, granted—exorbitant on the sidehills,
most of the leaves incandescent, drifting or plunging downward
to scuttle along the roadbeds like little creatures reluctant
to be seen, yet wanting us to notice them after all.

But give me this: middle November, season of sticks,
of stubborn oak and beech leaves, umber and dun, which rattle
in gusts that smell so elemental they stab your heart.
The trees—the other, unclothed ones—are standing there,
gaunt but dignified, and you can look straight past them
to the contours of the mountains, stark, perhaps, but lovely

in their apparent constancy. That gap-toothed barn
houses space alone since its owner died. Do you remember
Studebakers? That's one over there, a pickup truck,
flat-footed among the sumacs. Painted green way back,
these days it has taken the hue of these later leaves I love.
Old age has changed the mountains too. They're rounder now

than once, shaped so by the eons. Everything's for a time.

Solace, Stone

—1981

I had lately known a real grief:
my young brother—gone. So I set out alone.
Deep in Breaux's Gore, where I'd never been
until that morning, a headstone leaned.

It was quiet. There was never such quiet.
Who can recall that marker but me?
Who is there even to know about it?
Doubtless someone. Hunters must see

the canted slab now and then,
there since 1841.
It only bore one name: *John Goodridge*,
maybe wife- and childless. Water and sun

had worn its shoulders smooth.
Home late afternoon, near evening,
I moved from woodpile to shed and back,
less as if I were working than dreaming.

Scents rose in that autumn dusk,
then settled. Odors of wood and rain.

I settled too, in the wheelbarrow's bed,
like a shard of log, or some mud, or a stone

that might passively ride along.
Forty years gone by since I bore witness
to that marker, the world around me turned mute.
I'd never known so entire a silence.

I wouldn't forget it. Not ever.
I would never not hear that stillness again.
Our little family was set for winter.
We'd soon be soothed by the iron stove's hum.

I turned from our surfeit of firewood,
And felt at once that a gentle something—
from above the trees that loomed by the woodshed
and down through leaf and needle—was falling

into my bone, my flesh.
I thought back on that morning, laden with silence,
as if I could move beyond joy or sadness,
stone-quiet myself, and this could mean solace.

The Seafarer

—on the anniversary of my father's death

Technically, Marcus drowned in the fluid that flooded his lungs.
So I heard from a friend, his nurse. She told me he'd never wed.
So no wife. No child. Except for that nurse, he died alone.
Then some lawyer called, describing how Marcus had been as a kid:

"Normal—until they yanked his tonsils out." The ether
In overdose drenched his brain. Eight years old. Too late,
My friend grasped why his words came like sounds from underwater,
Why for Marcus the rules of Bingo were so hard to navigate.

His nurse had wrongly imagined the man retarded, or *challenged,*
To use her euphemism. Whatever you'd call it, he met
His problem head-on. He worked for years at a bakeshop in Boston,
Then drifted north seeking harbor, which, given his case, turned out

To be our local church home. The town librarian here
Brought him books. He liked to read about boats—but "wood ones only,
Not those messes made of metal." His yen for old ships must have squared
With what little my friend later learned of his father's career in the Navy,

Which ended when storm swept him off a cold steel deck to a grave
In the ocean. He wore a look at times that puzzled the staff,
Though they came to recognize it, tears coming in virtual waves
From his anxious eyes. And what, to witness that sort of grief,

92

Did the medical people imagine?   Having nothing but their descriptions,
I conjure young Marcus myself: he brushes the flour from his hands,
Then walks a few blocks to the bay,   where he gazes at ships in the distance,
The new metal kind, no doubt.   I picture him as he scans

The prospect, squinting to make   bright spars and planks appear,
Along with windlass and capstan,   and himself standing tall at a tiller.
A fatherland's out there somewhere.   Calm and intent, he steers
Toward what he's construed from books   or his own inner visions. However,

Something in me is looking   for a similar hint at redemption.
I didn't know Marcus at all.   This is second-hand elegy,
So I know it's only presumption   to make of him a steersman,
As if such longing belonged   to him alone, not me.

Dark Chord

—remembering Jack Myers (2011)

Some hours before I drove there, I slipped the DVD
of *Mingus in Europe* into the player, and there he was
on bass, with Eric Dolphy on alto and bass clarinet,
Jaki Byard on keyboard, Dannie Richmond, drums,
Johnny Coles on trumpet, and Clifford Jordan, tenor.
They looked so young and strong. They were so gifted, and I was here

on a jetty above the Atlantic, one of several friends
and family gathered to scatter the ashes of Jack, our poet,
into the waves. Poor Eric Dolphy died within months
of that tour in '64 while I finished up my chaotic
college years. I'd been no genius, I'd had so little
to offer the world, but there I was now. A pair of cormorants

skimmed quickly by while two young lovers embraced the way
they're supposed to embrace on the beach, and I saw the moon rise full.
All was perfect, it seemed—except that Jack wasn't with us.
Which may have accounted for the sound: not the intricate magic
of that Mingus band I heard, nor a line or a stanza from Jack's
mournful, witty, brilliant poems. Nor was it the cry

of sea birds. If Wagner didn't drive me almost mad,
or maybe because he *does*, I'd have said that the chord was a dark

94

Wagnerian one. As it played it washed all over me
as surf does a rocky shore. Some aunt or cousin that evening
would show me a picture of Jack at seventeen right here
in Winthrop, Massachusetts—sitting, cocky and proud,

on a motorcycle, handsome and frank, and it was oddly as though
I somehow heard that photograph too. Jack sounded so young.
His engine rumbled while he said something in that Boston brogue
he never lost. A boyhood friend had a word or two
to say as well, but broke down before he could finish. *I'll miss him
terribly,* said Mark, sweet mutual friend. And terrible

it might be, so when I heard the chord again it reminded me—
as I fought for balance on those rough and slippery rocks because
I was old, Jack's age exactly, damn it. I was older than
those masters of jazz holding forth in Europe, vibrant, alive,
back in a year when I was only 21:
the chord reminded me—as I noted the cormorants

winging back and the lovers walking back, and the moon,
and noted the ocean breeze of good Jack's Winthrop childhood,
and thought I could be noting all this idly, as believe me
in this moment I'd love to have done—the dark chord reminded me *Something
big has been shaping up for years and years and now
you know, old man, it's for all of us here, including you.*

Easy Wonder

—*Oxbrook Lake, July 2014*

My love, we floated for hours
in kayaks, side by side, scarcely dipping our paddles.
No motors allowed here, no soul in any
of the southerly shore's three other cabins.

Still, we orbited north,
through a calm, sequestered cove, where beavers had left
musked piles of mud on four flat rocks.
We didn't smell fetor: the breeze bore it off.

The beavers somehow know
to place their mounds at every point of the compass.
We wondered how they could be so precise,
though ours, to be sure, was easy wonder.

The same breeze lifts the curtain
in our room, from which we've banished watches and clocks,
having no obligations, our children grown,
they and their children not due here for weeks.

The wind raises tendrils of hair
from your pillowed head. How I adore your hair.
The water, quiet marvel, appeared to lift us
above all tension, above despair

at those wrenching deaths last year,
your mother's and brother's, and whatever else could appall.
You trailed an arm in the water. I love
your arms, and your legs, which were tucked in the hull.

As if fixed in one place, the sun
shed just the right warmth on us as it floated there.
We floated too, between water and air,
as if we'd never be let down.

The View in Late Winter

—*for Stephen Arkin*

My wife and one of our daughters, home to visit,
sleep through the creaks and moans of timber and sill.
More than I might have once, I welcome
warmth, so I drop in a log.
One fights the tug of nostalgia,
fights to accept the idea of acceptance,
of surrendering first one thing, then others, then all.

To judge by the journal I just took down from a shelf,
on this very day in 1968,
I hiked all the way up Mousely Mountain
to camp at height of land.
There are maybe a dozen visions
etched forever into my mind,
and one, however minor, is of that night,

when the world seemed oddly, generously upside down.
From high above them, I spied on a pair of owls
that coasted tree to tree below,
while their perfect shadows below them
slid over snow, cast there
by a moon as wrought as museum marble,
all else but those birds and shadows supremely still.

I just inspected the mercury through a frosted pane:
at 22 below, it seems far too frigid
to scrape the ashes out of the firebox.
I should have done so before
this cold snap, but that would have meant
letting the stove go dead to haul them,
and thus to invite the chill into our kitchen.

Instead of moon or predator or hill,
from a favorite chair beside the stove I fix on
a lovely ceramic plate we found
in an Umbrian village somewhere.
Our honeymoon. Years ago. . . .
On the cluttered counter before it stand
still photographs of children and their children.

I see pictures as well of dogs, most of them gone.
Each thing in anyone's life is fated to go,
though here it comes, the faithful day.
I long, however vainly,
for what I have loved to stay.
Another photo shows our house by the pond,
with its still, inverted reflection in water below.

Some Postures toward the Rock

—for Sissy Boyd, dancer

i. Rock, Boy

He's at an age where it feels less real,
this massive rock,
than the half-dozen whiskered, goat-eyed catfish
that gasp in his bag.

Noon stands gazing down at him.
Grasshoppers scratch
in weeds going to seed. He grips his twitching
sack of trophies,

collects his can of worms, his pole,
and finds a seat.
He's pleased with his life, unaware of the rock,
how it warms and supports him.

ii. Rock, Dog

Trotting the road on the bias, he freezes,
taking the rock
for fun: bird, squirrel, woodchuck.
Flattened to earth,

he begins his stalk. Light sneaks through the woods
and reaches the stone.
He takes the shine for fur or hide,
champs and trembles.

He charges, but the charge dies off and fades
into unfocused gazing.
He snuffs, lifts a leg, then languidly wanders
among brown meadows.

iii. Rock, Madman

An owl, he thinks, hooted this rock
into being. Mouse-bones
dot the chalk that the bird dropped there.
With a long enough pole

he might pry the rock, then throw himself under.
Too late, too late:
small skeletons, cartilage, eyeballs, fur
hop back into place,

the rodents scatter as the owl sails in.
Hey nonny, nonny. . . .
The raptor's an omen, he believes, of storm,
or something worse.

101

iv. Rock, Liar

Twilight arrives. The rock's still there
where nature dropped it,
though he's always claimed it was he who placed it,
the rock impressive

as he yearns to be. There's no time now
for the rest of life.
He and that slab must not be seen
with one another

lest someone bid him, *Lift it now.*
If only they'd die,
the ones he bragged to! Perhaps he could move it,
or end his existence.

v. Rock, Dancer

The rock has made its huge dent in turf.
She thinks that an age's
rain might wash it down to pebble.
The hole would remain.

She should have been an engineer,
or *something sensible,*
as her parents urged. This is despair.
An orange moon crowns

and she doesn't care. So is it mere habit
that summons the music?
She whirls until pale lichens grow lovely
on the beautiful rock,

and the moon turns rosy.

V. Gift

Who Knows? That Lifelong Question

i. He Risks a Walk

Between two pock-marked beech, on a strand of wire
For another era's cows, the cruel barbs shine,
Blossoms of brightness. When darkness stoops, Orion
Will shine likewise, as always, among the stars.
He'll nock his arrow, as if to kindle mayhem
Below. For now, the old man thinks of the house,
Where his wife may still feel fretful. The weather scared them
Last night with sideways rain, which in due course froze.
When he all but trips on a winter-kill, he wonders,
Has he read somewhere of a people who buried their dead
As the grouse in his path is buried, neck and head
Alone protruding, or was that just some old torture?
The plump bird's ruff is burnished by the frost.

The poor thing had hidden in powder. When snow turned to ice,
It sealed the body in. So peculiar a sight
Has stopped the old man cold in this foolish walk.
Today's no day for wandering under trees,
Going off everywhere around him, loud as guns,
All clap and crack in bursting limbs and trunks.
Sunbeams garland the forest in silvery beads,
Every branch and bole, both shattered and whole,
A radiant filament. He can't figure why

Death looks so brilliant. Its dead eyes rimed and white,
That head might be a flower, or maybe a jewel
Carelessly dropped by somebody roaming here
Where the walker feels his way, the trail so sheer.

ii. He Walks and Stops

His trail so sheer, his knees not what they were,
The walker finds himself
Pausing more often than stepping, and in these lulls—
Although he's tired of memory,
Damnable habit that's been the stuff of his life—
The past creeps up again.

He muses how it's the biggest surprise he's known:
The fact that he's gotten old,
That, for example, he's forced to put a hand
On each of his creaky knees
And push down hard whenever he needs to step up
Onto even slight swells or rock-forms.

It's what he did, he recalls, on grammar-school stairs,
And then, in adolescence,
Went on to mock the younger boys for doing.
He sees those small ones still,
Their untucked shirts and trousers and untied shoes
Gone muddy out on the playground.

As they pant on the steps, their little mouths agape,
The dread, imperious bell

Reminds them that they're late again. They're late.
The old man also sees
In this red oak grove a few stumps here and there
Of long-gone trees he hewed

Thirty years back or more, their wood turned dozy,
Such that he all but pictures
Their turning to air itself were he to kick them,
Although of course he won't,
For fear of losing balance. Imagination,
Vision—it's all he has,

It seems, by which he means the ceaseless function
Of selective memory.
He thinks of war in the Mideast now, for instance,
And thinks he ought to be thinking
Of that, or of any news his mother described
In his boyhood as *current events,*

Rebuking his idle dreaming. He hears her opinion
To this day and can't gainsay it.
Three cord in eight short hours: that's what he'd fell
And cut and split and stack.
Why shouldn't he still be strong? Another surprise.
He walks on fifty feet

And pauses once again. A random gust
Stirs up a scent of winter.
He can't identify it, though it's familiar:
He's taken this odor in
For seven decades, but now he wants to ignore it.
He'd rather not be mired

For so much as a moment in even the least old question.
Yet how does one look ahead
Or out from here? The prospect appears absurd.
For all of that, he notes
The buds of February tending to purple
The way they've always done,

And he has to conjure spring. There's nothing for it,
He simply can't resist.
Is this mere habit too, or might it be
An authentic sense of revival?
He walks a while again and stops again,
Walks on and doesn't know.

iii. He'll Stay With That

He doesn't know as he walks
That two coyotes are mating
In that late-growth fir clump northward,
Within yards of where he passes.

.

He knows just enough to imagine
They're there. If he comes again
In eight or nine weeks, the bitch
Will howl, if she exists.

She'll be guarding her whelps from the walker
Unless or until he moves on.
If she feels fear, she'll hide it.
Ice down on the river

Will have loosened up its suction
To either shore, and he
May not witness this either. Who knows?
Who knows? That lifelong question.

He tries not to prophesy
What constitutes his future,
Urging himself instead
To consider what little he *can* know,

Or at least can see. For instance,
These tiny, wriggling specks
In the granular stuff under trees:
Snow fleas, harbingers

Of the sugar maker's season.
Perhaps he'll stay with that,
Will end with sweet figuration
As home rises into sight.

October Moon on Lake

Not another poem about a stunning moon!
It won't be me who writes it.
I've heard the clichés, I've seen that shine so often,
there's nothing more to mean,
to see or say. And yet at that you ought to behold

this pair of night-time loons,
for instance, paddling through a riffled band of light
the moon has deftly laid
from that far shore to this. There may be more to come,
probably more to be told,

even more to signify. It's just that I,
feeling awkward, oblique, can't figure
how or what or why, no matter that now I consider
the cavortings over the sky
to my east of that trio of swallows, who might have returned to their holes,

twilight turning to dark,
to wherever they go after they've played themselves out.
They would have done so, no doubt,
had the moon under which they caper not been so immense,
so vivid, so candid, so bold.

Snapper

It seems a greater wonder that I should have made it
through my boyhood years than that the lone dark snapper
who skulked in my uncle's springhouse survived as well.
I tried to blow its head off all one summer,
my puny .22's wild bullets glancing
from its carapace and then—*zing-zing*—off water,
sill and stone. The turtle may well have been eighty:

those old pirates live for ages and ages.
From the pterodactyls' time, their race has lingered.
I was 12 or 13 myself. You can't die either
if you're that young, no more than your mother or father,
extinction some faraway nation that no one visits.
For convenience, I'll call the snapper *him* hereafter.
This one's mate, or mates, dwelled somewhere else.

In June those females often laid their eggs
in the gravel bank on the other side of the pond,
but they could have done so any time of year
before hard frost. At length their tiny spawn
would shuck their shells and scrabble for open water.
Most were doubtless gobbled up by coon
or fox or mink or crow or dog or heron.

As for me back then, it was righteousness I aimed at.
I never thought of my quarry as something I'd eat,
though I greedily slurped up snapper soup years later
after bone-chilling days on the Chesapeake hunting geese.
And I never wondered where that quarry might go
come dead of winter. By then my play had ceased:
I was stuck at school, where Johnny Silver ruled.

He bounced dirt clods or snowballs off my body
at every recess. All I could do was flee him,
or try to hide until I heard the bell.
I didn't visit the springhouse in that season.
There was homework, nightly, noisy, clannish suppers,
awakening of pubescence's unreason,
awkwardness of unfamiliar lust.

I'd come now and then on snappers up on land,
bumbling, clumsy, but I was disinclined
to shoot them there, though I took mean joy in teasing
hisses from them with whatever I could find.
I remember one's breaking the shaft of a broom I wielded,
but I knew he'd never catch me if he tried.
A snapping turtle's slower than slow on ground,

yet his normal heart rate is 200 beats a minute—
until, that is, he sinks into mud for winter.
Then the rate, astoundingly, drops to two a day.
He endures on body fat alone, the snapper,
staving off acidosis by the leaching
of carbonates from his shell. He's simply a wonder!
It doesn't matter what we humans think,

whether he strikes us as loathsome, as he did me
when to murder one seemed a noble thing to do,
a little part I could play in the world's salvation.
This much later, I wince at nightly news:
I see beheadings, I hear of unmanned bombers
sent to crush what the second Bush, that fool,
described as evil-doers. We know we're righteous

and feel free therefore to eradicate whole towns
as surely as predators ravage newborn snappers.
I somehow survive. I never shot myself,
no more than I shot a slug through that quiet glider—
the one who haunted my uncle's springhouse waters,
who in my childish eye embodied evil,
and whom, though I didn't know it, I risked my life for.

Earth and Heaven

My wife has already changed and gone
to work. Retired, I have time to consider
the smell of her cheek when she came indoors
from this morning's chill. Can there be a heaven?
If so, it will hang in the air, that odor.
I'm not alone.

I have dear friends of a certain age
who scan the notices of death
like me, first thing, in the local paper,
comparing the age of the vanished with theirs.
We reckon the years we likely have left.
A good, full life—

that's the cliché for those gone at 80.
I'm 70-plus. I'd also expect
babblings in heaven from some of our seven
grandchildren, who'd also still gather with us.
Their antics, embraces, and wise-guy remarks
would all still bless me.

I swear to God: Mortality,
I don't fear you. What I'll leave is what troubles,
including just now the two best dogs
we've owned, however we loved the rest.

Male pointer and female retriever nestle
tight by the woodstove.

It's 20 below. Outside, three songbirds
jostle the feeder, which spills seeds on snow.
We can see, in such clear and brilliant weather,
all the way to the mountains, the rugged Whites
beyond the river. My wife and I love
to walk along

that totemic flow, looking into New Hampshire.
Yesterday, after thaw and freeze,
the streambed's ice chunks slapped back the sun
like gigantic gems. Lately I've thought
I ought to revise all my poetry
from an earlier time.

Who failed to be a little naïve
when young? There's so much now I couldn't foretell.
I'd scarcely dreamed children, let alone their children.
I tell myself now: Look out the window.
It's a late-winter Monday, stunningly cold,
in the Year of Our Lord

2018. The poor deer must keep moving
for fear of freezing if they pause too long.
Her ten-month-old twin offspring behind her,
a sleek doe tiptoes down our drive.
Three silhouettes against whited lawn.
It's been a hard winter,

with more to come, yet they look so alive.

Zero Fahrenheit

Tugged by the notion of strong black coffee,
I get out of bed and embrace my wife.
About time. The dogs lie tight to the stove.
All three look eager to climb right inside.

She has walked them already and dished their food.
I hear the chuckle of kindling cedar:
She's been reviving the fire while I clove
To my quilts, a common, self-seeking behavior.

Together we study an upriver eagle,
Backlit, unmoving, on a dark arm of pine.
The stream whispers too. But for red squirrels' scribblings,
The snow shows pluperfectly blank. Still it shines.

The woman glows also, even the lines
Between eyebrows. Those tracings—she's earned every one,
Having stood close by me no matter my failings,
Having borne and instructed daughters and sons.

I know that today is all we own,
None of us leaving the planet alive.
Against logic, however, I dream guarantees—
That our eagle, for instance, will pose against sky

On that pine bough forever, that the three dogs will lie
By the hearth, that I'll be able to cherish
My wife as I do, but perennially,
That the woods will show powder, whose bright white won't perish.

On My Love of Country Life

The question may be raised why we
chose precisely the past of a city to
compare with the past of a mind.
—Civilization and Its Discontents

He ruminated, cigar in crippled jaw.
Cocaine pulsed like the strobe on that cop's parked cruiser.
There's oceanic distance from where Freud sat
To where I stand just now as I visit Manhattan,
Which back in the doctor's day was no Big Apple.
The Sheep Meadow still held sheep. But in time they'd vanish,

This park would be thronged, and we would raise his question—
Or I would, comparing his moment to our own,
When even that rim of posies by the reservoir's
South end at 87th seems a threat.
Imagination, mine at least, would crave
A village, clean, essential, if maybe not

The one I've lived in so long. Are you like me?
Can you conjure some antique European hamlet,
Complete with organ grinder, antic monkey,
Coins chink-chinking into a proffered cup,
Air as soft as bedclothes? Here in the city,
That bus's diesel chokes me. Jackhammers rattle,

Even past dark. Slate pigeons move at will,
Cosmopolites, while the park affects a show
Of green among the cans and candy wrappers,
Rinds and condoms, jugs of Sneaky Pete
In shards. The traffic seems deployed for battle.
Its headlamps will sweep across the stoops come night,

Across the benches, where mad folk rage against
The day gone by, or sports teams, politicians.
Just so, at night, some of us heard the elders,
Late in our anxious puberty. They shrieked
Their calumnies downstairs. They slammed odd doors.
Are you like me? Did you long for simple precision,

Some scrap of explanation? Why do I keep
Including you? You may not be like me,
Who craved it so for all those years and years—
A way I could make some sense of the inward city.
Not that I thought in those terms, and even then,
My mind ached likewise for another place,
Where things grew blurry: a fleece-like nap of meadow,
The spring blooms' brightness muted, peasant wagons
Full of hay gone fragrant with evening, the glow

Of a vanishing sun on the picturesque houses' stone,
And cattle and sheep intent upon their grazing—
Their grazing placid, narcotic, every moment

Much like the one before, their mild jaws rolling.

To a Granddaughter in My Arms

I can't play Duck-Duck-Goose anymore,
I tell you—barely four years old,
And feather-light in my arms. I might
Try joining you in the family's game,
But it takes me so long now to stand from sitting
I'd lose every round—but you might like that,
Victory still all harmless delight

For you, not an urge for arrogant triumph,
Not lust for another's humiliation.
Why can't you do it, Grandpa? you ask.
I shrug and say, *I'm old.* Outside,
Late March, the hills still showing snow,
Though out the south window as I stand here and hold you,
I notice green hinting itself in the grass,

The dun stubble fading, and downhill, pines
Flaring with incandescent candles.
Spring growth. Yes, sweetheart, I'm simply too old
For your harmless play, and you can't see
What I see all over—the sweet and the other.
One day you will, but Lord knows there's no hurry.
Things make their rounds. So do we all.

Mindfulness

For some it's prayer and for others I guess it's sitting quiet zazen
And for others still it's chanting a litany of protest
At what life deals them and though I pray myself in my way
I've been known to recite the litany too though it's clear I do best
When I go downstairs and make a cup of strong black coffee

In the elegant glass French press my wife so good and lovely gave me
Years ago I think for one or another birthday
Then drink it because I should desire to be awake
To the world I see around me though it's more than merely coffee
That will make me so I understand but still and all

The ritual can help incline my stubborn heart and soul
To appreciate that a doe let's say before she runs
Stands silhouetted sideways there on the ridge outside
Our window momentarily backlit by morning sun
And I should treasure the ridge itself and all the rest

The sun included spangling all this myriad glorious mess
Of October color which I'm willing to grant is just as corny
As any postcard but I also believe that for me to treat it
As no more than trite will mean to miss the point entirely
Of why I should sustain deep gratitude no matter

Autumn's here and gone more quickly nowadays than ever
Though that should be even greater cause for me to marvel
At all I behold and never mind that I don't sit
Like some wise monk or yogi or sage I can nonetheless be mindful
Feeling that certain inclination that only a cretin

Would fail to cherish so why should I not feel it more often

Gift

Some weeks ago, it looked as though
Sparse snow had fallen in a straight line beside
The lane where we walk our dogs. That seemed odd.

It was only the year's wild strawberry blossoms.
Today, that small drift vanished again,
The fruit is ready for reaping. But then

How little one gathers for the effort involved!
The berries, more hull than meat, are stingy,
And my back is creaky, and my fingers are clumsy.

When our children were small they could sometimes be chores—
Beautiful chores, but chores nonetheless.
Now we'd have them back. They grew up so fast.

Ten minutes of picking, scanty harvest.
It seems, as my grandmother used to mutter,
Not worth the candle, though no candle is called for,

The late-spring morning crisp and alive,
Lit by a thousand thousand greens
From the arch of trees, and no matter I lean

A bit at the waist, having stooped to my task
For meager reward, when I reach our door
My matchless wife is standing there.

My wife, open-armed, at an open door.

Here Itself

. . . eluting stent placed in occluded right coronary artery of otherwise
fit and pleasant 73-year-old male, former poet laureate of Vermont.
—*from Eastern Maine Medical Center patient's report, 8/21/2016.*

i.

I had a heart attack *is something,*
I kept on thinking,
one hears from others.

In search of dazzling revelation,
I'd wandered blind through the world,
had begun to see as much.

Having approached Paul's barbershop
For instance down the same asphalt alley
In the same old hardscrabble hamlet

And through the same old waiting room
With those copies, unchanging, of Guns and Ammo,
Popular Mechanics—*what have you?*—

I contemplated the ancient jug of Lucky Tiger,
Paul's horseshoe-pitching trophies,
The snapshot, curling around its tacks,

Of the 350-pound bear at his feeder.
And Paul. And myself. Right there in the mirror,
As ever. It's thirty years and more

He's been cutting my hair
As it's dwindled. Three full decades
Of identical questions when he's nearing the finish.

Wet or dry?
Shall I do the eyebrows?
A little more off the top?
Trim the ears?

Of course he knows the answers.
It's a rite, is all—and a very comfort.
Wonder lies in minuscule things.

I'm here.

     ii.

There's a tough late solitary dahlia
In our flower garden.

A hooded merganser drake is grating

Like a rusted hinge from our pond.
I notice these things
As it seems to me now I haven't before.

I felt no fear, just wistfulness—
For wife, children, grandchildren, friends.

I had a dress rehearsal for death,
But no, no terror.

Strapped to a gurney, I went off to visit
The Wonderful Isness of Was,

The Isness of Forever.

iii.

An Indian Summer paddle trip
On my beloved Connecticut River:
Reflected below, crows cross the water
To disappear behind a scrim
Of yellow leaves. Cottonwood. Silver maple.
I can't quite describe it, but here I am to see it.

I push through the windrows of lustrous fall foliage
On the surface. There,
Above the village steeple,
A cloud, resembling nothing, only itself.
Not chastity, not purity, cotton, whipped cream.
Itself. Who'd want it other? I'm here

To see it. Itself, entire.

Acknowledgments

The author thanks editors of the following periodicals, in which most of these poems first appeared, sometimes in moderately different form:

American Literary Journal, Agni, Boulevard, Four Way Review, the *Georgia Review,* the *Hopper, The Hudson Review, Mud Season Review, New Ohio Review, Northern Woodlands, Numéro Cinq, Plume, Salmagundi,* and the *Southern Review*

Inexpressible thanks also to my faithful critics, supporters, and dear friends Fleda Brown, Stephen Arkin, Marjan Strojan, and, as ever, my wife Robin—matchless, all right.

Sydney Lea, a former Pulitzer finalist, founded and for thirteen years edited *New England Review*. This is his thirteenth poetry collection and his twentieth book. He will soon publish *The Music of What Happens: Lyric and Everyday Life*, his collected newspaper columns from his years (2011-15) as Vermont Poet Laureate. His collaborative book of essays with former Delaware laureate Fleda Brown, *Growing Old in Poetry: Two Poets, Two Lives*, appeared in 2018. He has been active in literacy efforts and conservation, especially in Maine, where the land trust he chaired until 2018 conserved nearly 400,000 acres of working forest.

Publication of this book was made possible by grants and donations. We are also grateful to those individuals who participated in our 2018 Build a Book Program. They are:

Anonymous (11), Vincent Bell, Jan Bender-Zanoni, Laurel Blossom, Adam Bohanon, Lee Briccetti, Jane Martha Brox, Carla & Steven Carlson, Andrea Cohen, Janet S. Crossen, Marjorie Deninger, Patrick Donnelly, Charles Douthat, Blas Falconer, Monica Ferrell, Joan Fishbein, Jennifer Franklin, Sarah Freligh, Helen Fremont & Donna Thagard, Robert Fuentes & Martha Webster, Ryan George, Panio Gianopoulos, Lauri Grossman, Julia Guez, Naomi Guttman & Jonathan Mead, Steven Haas, Bill & Cam Hardy, Lori Hauser, Ricardo Hernandez, Bill Holgate, Deming Holleran, Piotr Holysz, Nathaniel Hutner, Rebecca Kaiser Gibson, Voki Kalfayan, David Lee, Sandra Levine, Howard Levy, Owen Lewis, Jennifer Litt, Sara London & Dean Albarelli, David Long, Ralph & Mary Ann Lowen, Jacquelyn Malone, Fred Marchant, Louise Mathias, Catherine McArthur, Nathan McClain, Richard McCormick, Kamilah Aisha Moon, Beth Morris, Rebecca & Daniel Okrent, Jill Pearlman, Marcia & Chris Pelletiere, Maya Pindyck, Megan Pinto, Eileen Pollack, Barbara Preminger, Kevin Prufer, Martha Rhodes, Paula Rhodes, Linda Safyan, Peter & Jill Schireson, Jason Schneiderman, Roni & Richard Schotter, Jane Scovel, Andrew Seligsohn & Martina Anderson, Soraya Shalforoosh, Julie A. Sheehan, James Snyder & Krista Fragos, Alice St. Claire-Long, Megan Staffel, Dorothy Tapper Goldman, Marjorie & Lew Tesser, Boris Thomas, Connie Voisine, Calvin Wei, Bill Wenthe, Allison Benis White, Michelle Whittaker, Rachel Wolff, and Anton Yakovlev.